*This book was a gift
to our library
from Capstone Press.*

# We Need Teachers

### by Jane Scoggins Bauld

Consulting Editor: Gail Saunders-Smith, Ph.D.

Consultant: Max Laird, President,
North Dakota Education Association

## Pebble Books

an imprint of Capstone Press
Mankato, Minnesota

Pebble Books are published by Capstone Press
151 Good Counsel Drive, P.O. Box 669, Mankato, Minnesota 56002
http://www.capstone-press.com

2 3 4 5 6 05 04 03 02 01

Library of Congress Cataloging-in-Publication Data
Bauld, Jane Scoggins.
    We need teachers/by Jane Scoggins Bauld.
    p. cm.—(Helpers in our school)
    Includes bibliographical references and index.
    Summary: Simple text and photographs present teachers and their
elementary schools.
    ISBN 0-7368-0533-8
    1. Teachers—Juvenile literature. [1. Teachers. 2. Occupations.] I. Titl
LB1775 .B364   2000
372.11—dc21                                              99-046802

# Note to Parents and Teachers

The Helpers in Our School series supports national social studies
standards for how groups and institutions work to meet individual
needs. This book describes teachers and illustrates what they do in
schools. The photographs support early readers in understanding
the text. The repetition of words and phrases helps early readers
learn new words. This book also introduces early readers to subject-
specific vocabulary words, which are defined in the Words to Know
section. Early readers may need assistance to read some words and
to use the Table of Contents, Words to Know, Read More, Internet
Sites, and Index/Word List sections of the book.

# Table of Contents

Teachers help
students learn.

Teachers set up
classrooms.

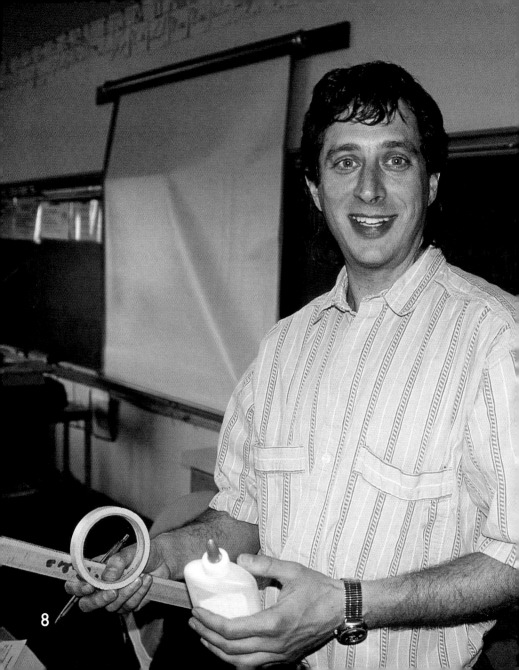

8

Teachers gather supplies.

Teachers plan lessons.

Teachers grade homework.

Some teachers teach
one subject.

Some teachers teach many subjects.

Teachers help students work together.

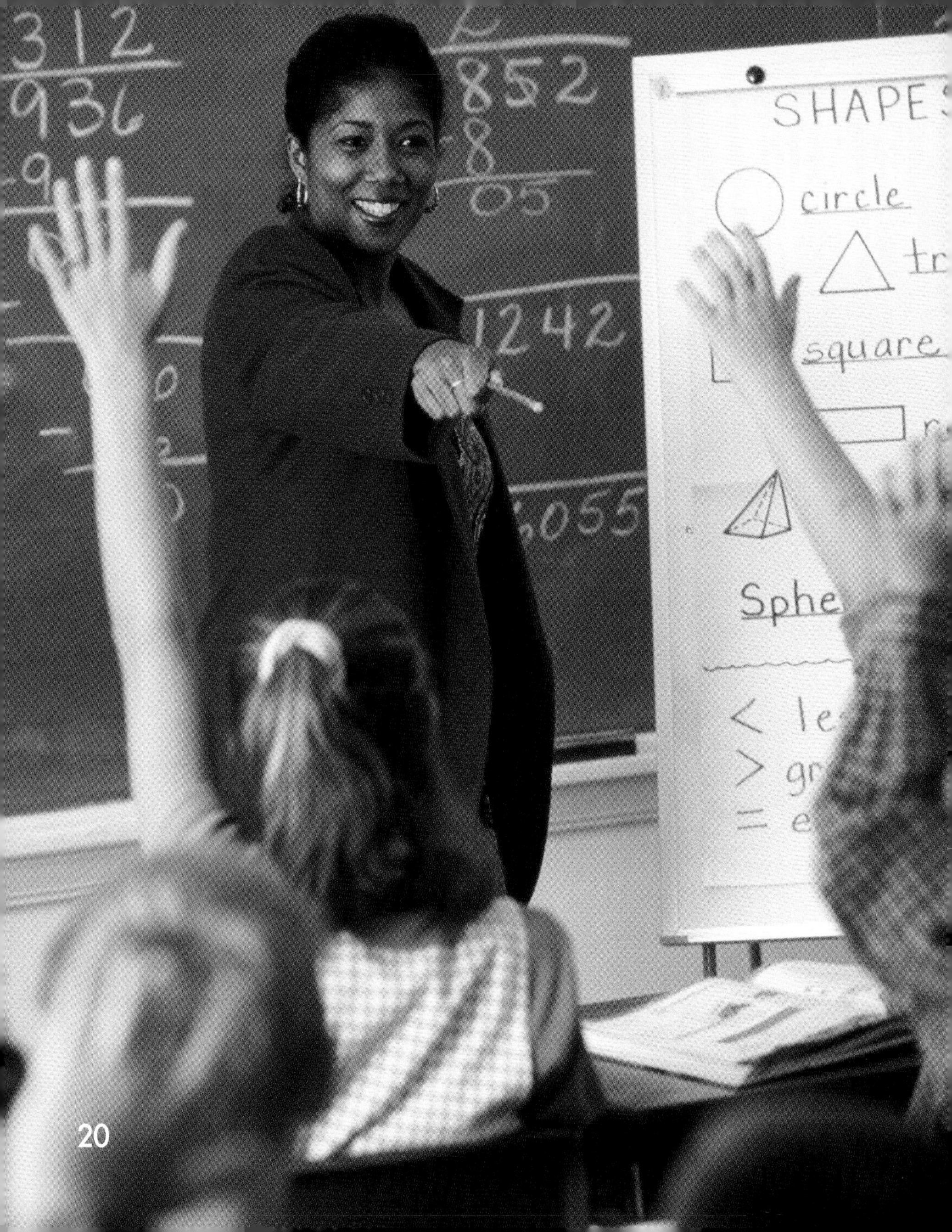
SHAPES
circle
square

Teachers help students want to learn.

# Words to Know

**classroom**—a room in a school where classes take place; some teachers teach in one classroom and others teach in many classrooms.

**lesson**—a set of skills or facts taught at one time; teachers prepare lessons for each day of class.

**plan**—to decide how something will be done; teachers plan lessons and activities for students.

**student**—a person who goes to a school to learn; teachers help students learn.

**subject**—an area of study such as reading, mathematics, or history

**supplies**—items needed to perform a task; teachers have books, paper, computers, and other supplies in classrooms.

**teacher**—a person who helps others learn and solve problems; teachers encourage students to want to learn.

# Read More

Deedrick, Tami. *Teachers.* Community Helpers. Mankato, Minn.: Bridgestone Books, 1998.

Greene, Carol. *Teachers Help Us Learn.* Community Helpers. Chanhassen, Minn.: Child's World, 1998.

Weber, Valerie and Gloria Jenkins. *School in Grandma's Day.* In Grandma's Day. Minneapolis: Carolrhoda Books, 1999.

# Internet Sites

Family Education Network
http://familyeducation.com

Jobs for Kids Who Like Reading
http://stats.bls.gov/k12/html/edu_read.htm

Only a Teacher
http://www.pbs.org/onlyateacher

What Teachers Do
http://www.whatdotheydo.com/teacher.htm

# Index/Word List

**Word Count: 38**
**Early-Intervention Level: 7**

**Editorial Credits**

Martha E. H. Rustad, editor; Abby Bradford, Bradfordesign, Inc., cover designer; Kia Bielke, production designer; Kimberly Danger, photo researcher

**Photo Credits**

International Stock/George Ancona, 14, 16
Jim Cummins/FPG International LLC, cover
Kim Stanton, 6, 8
Mark Adams/FPG International LLC, 20
Shaffer Photography/James L. Shaffer, 18
Unicorn Stock Photos/Jeff Greenberg, 10; Martin Jones, 12
Uniphoto/Bob Daemmrich, 4
Visuals Unlimited/Nancy Alexander, 1